Scan this QR code
to read online!

Unveiling Deceit

Marcus, a dedicated father and prosperous entrepreneur, was eagerly preparing for a well-deserved vacation. He meticulously planned a two-week excursion to Rio De Janeiro for himself and his children. Marcus was particularly keen on spending quality time with his son, King, and his daughter, Kiki.

While Marcus was finalizing the travel plans, his ex-wife, Elizabeth, suddenly unveiled her coinciding travel plans. This triggered a series of misunderstandings, and Marcus couldn't help but question the timing of her trip. Marcus was concerned with who was going to be keeping King while both were going to be out of the country. Elizabeth told him that her mother would watch him so Marcus was relieved.

Marcus was having a wonderful time on the trip. Things took an unexpected twist when Elizabeth accused Marcus of inappropriate content on King's tablet. Marcus could not believe it because he was out of the country at the time. Marcus was shocked. He had given King the tablet purely for learning purposes so he wouldn't be bored knowing that both parents would be out of the country at the same time so Marcus was adamant about his innocence.

Despite Marcus's denials, Elizabeth escalated the issue to court, jeopardizing their co-parenting arrangement. This led Marcus to seek the help of Kiesha Howard, a highly recommended attorney. Kiesha Howard was a well-dressed attorney she really had a fashion sense. People from all over Baltimore knew who she was. Actually, she is the person who recommended Amber Jackson who is no longer able to represent Marcus considering she was elected to a judge's seat.

As Kiesha began building Marcus's defense, she discovered inconsistencies in Elizabeth's claims. The so-called inappropriate content was only vied by Elizabeth. it was discovered that King had not even accessed any apps on the tablet and that it all was a farce. The whole ordeal was orchestrated by Elizabeth to try and gain the upper hand because she didn't like the custody agreement. Marcus felt vindicated, but Kiesha advised him to remain patient.

The courtroom was filled with tension as Kiesha presented the evidence. Elizabeth's face turned pale when her deception was revealed. The court questioned her motives and integrity as a co-parent.

Despite the upcoming trial, Marcus was relieved that the situation didn't disrupt his quality time with King. He was grateful for Kiesha's unwavering dedication to justice. He reassured his children that their welfare would always be his priority.

Marcus vowed to be more vigilant about his and his children's privacy. Despite the adversities, he remained hopeful. He knew he would continue to fight for his rights as a father.

Finally, the ordeal was over, and Marcus, King, and Kiki could now look forward to their trip to Rio De Janeiro. Marcus promised them that he would take both of them with him on the next trip to Rio. Amidst the trials, they had emerged stronger and closer as a family.

The End.